HIP-HOP & R&B

Culture, Music & Storytelling

Post Malone

HIP-HOP & R&B

Culture, Music & Storytelling

Beyonce

Bruno Mars

Cardi B

Chance the Rapper

DJ Khaled

Drake

Jay-Z

John Legend

Lil Wayne

Nicki Minaj

Pharrell

Pitbull

Post Malone

Rihanna

The Weeknd

Travis Scott

MASON CREST

HIP-HOP & R&B

Post Malone

Culture, Music & Storytelling

MASON CREST

450 Parkway Drive, Suite D, Broomall, Pennsylvania 19008
(866) MCP-BOOK (toll-free) • www.masoncrest.com

Printed in the United States of America

First printing
9 8 7 6 5 4 3 2 1

ISBN (hardback) 978-1-4222-4367-1
ISBN (ebook) 978-1-4222-7446-0

Cataloging-in-Publication Data on file with the Library of Congress

NATIONAL HIGHLIGHTS

Developed and produced by National Highlights Inc.
Editor: Dave Johnstone
Production: Michelle Luke
Interior and cover design: Annalisa Gumbrecht, Studio Gumbrecht

QR CODES AND LINKS TO THIRD-PARTY CONTENT

CONTENTS

KEY ICONS TO LOOK OUT FOR:

Words to Understand: These words with their easy-to-understand definitions will increase the reader's understanding of the text while building vocabulary skills.

Sidebars: This boxed material within the main text allows readers to build knowledge, gain insights, explore possibilities, and broaden their perspectives by weaving together additional information to provide realistic and holistic perspectives.

Educational Videos: Readers can view videos by scanning our QR codes, providing them with additional educational content to supplement the text. Examples include news coverage, moments in history, speeches, iconic sports moments, and much more!

Text-Dependent Questions: These questions send the reader back to the text for more careful attention to the evidence presented there.

Research Projects: Readers are pointed toward areas of further inquiry connected to each chapter. Suggestions are provided for projects that encourage deeper research and analysis.

Series Glossary of Key Terms: This back-of-the-book glossary contains terminology used throughout this series. Words found here increase the reader's ability to read and comprehend higher-level books and articles in this field.

Post Malone
HIP-HOP & R&B

Career Highlights—
Setting Recording Industry Records

The hip-hop musician Post Malone, born Austin Richard Post, launched his career on SoundCloud, becoming one of the first artists to truly achieve success from self-publishing. His SoundCloud hit "White Iverson" thrust him onto the hip-hop scene. What could have insulted people instead amused them. The music community recognized that his schtick was a parody of early rappers, complete with the all-gold grill. Although his braids were real, he hails

Post Malone was born in Syracuse, New York, but was raised in Grapevine, Texas.

Scan to listen to
"Better Now."

from Syracuse, NY, by way of Grapevine, TX—
hardly a Compton-esque calling card.

He tattoos nearly every space on his body,
much like '80s heavy metal acts. His crew reminds
one of Kid Rock's homies. With a parody that
strong, he still did not market himself as a parody
act as did Weird Al Yankovic. While he writes his
lyrics in a serious vein, his delivery usually lacks
seriousness. That may be what saved him and
vaulted him up the charts. His SoundCloud
marketing brought him three hits from his debut
album on Republic Records. It was his follow-up
album, though, that set records.

All Released Solo Albums to Date:
Discography

STONEY
(Released December 9, 2016)

Malone's initial release spawned three hits,
"White Iverson," "Congratulations" and "I Fall Apart."
The artist co-produced his first hit single, "White
Iverson," with Rex Kudo, which charted at No. 14 on
the Billboard Top 40. His follow-up singles,
"Congratulations," and "I Fall Apart," also did well,
with the former certified diamond status, which
means ten times platinum by the Recording
Industry Association of America (RIAA), and the
latter charting as high as No. 16.

Justin Bieber collaborated with Post Malone on "Deja Vu" which features on the "Stoney" album.

Scan here to listen to "White Iverson," Malone's first hit that started out on SoundCloud.

STONEY *Album tracks*

1. **"Broken Whiskey Glass"**
2. **"Big Lie"**
3. **"Deja Vu"**
   (featuring Justin Bieber)
4. **"No Option"**
5. **"Cold"**
6. **"White Iverson"**
7. **"I Fall Apart"**
8. **"Patient"**
9. **"Go Flex"**
10. **"Feel"** (featuring Kehlani)
11. **"Too Young"**
12. **"Congratulations"**
    (featuring Quavo)
13. **"Up There"**
14. **"Yours Truly, Austin Post"**

Collaborations

- "Deja Vu," featuring Justin Bieber
- "Congratulations," featuring Quavo
- "Feel," featuring Kehlani

Rapper Quavo collaborated with Post Malone on "Congratulations" that is featured on the *Beerbongs & Bentleys* album.

Beerbongs & Bentleys
(Released April 27, 2018)

His sophomore Republic effort, *Beerbongs & Bentleys*, stormed the Billboard 200 in its release week and set a history-making record. Malone instantly claimed not only the no. 1 album chart spot, but thirteen more. Of the 18 songs on his follow up album, 14 instantly entered the Top 40.

Ty Dolla $ign collaborated with Post Malone on "Psycho" which features on the *Beerbongs & Bentleys* album.

It was the SoundCloud set again. Malone's streaming numbers vaulted him ahead of anything receiving AOR radio play. During its first week out, the 18 songs on the release received more than 430 million U.S. streams. The record-setting songs were:

No. 2	"Psycho," featuring Ty Dolla $ign
No. 7	"Better Now"
No. 8	"Rockstar," featuring 21 Savage

Scan here to listen to Post Malone's "Psycho" featuring Ty Dolla $ign.

21 Savage and Post Malone at the 2018
Billboard Awards.

No. 11   "Paranoid"

No. 14   "Rich & Sad"

No. 15   "Spoil My Night," featuring Swae Lee

No. 16   "Ball for Me," featuring Nicki Minaj

No. 17   "Stay"

No. 20   "Same Bitches," featuring G-Eazy & YG

No. 23   "Zack and Codeine"

No. 24   "Over Now"

No. 29   "Takin' Shots"

No. 34   "Candy Paint"

No. 40   "92 Explorer"

His record-breaking number of hits displaced rapper J. Cole as the former record holder. Cole had placed 10 songs in the Top 40 at once. Behind him ranked Cardi B, Drake, and Kendrick Lamar, who all at one time or another had nine hits in the Top 40 at one time.

Collaborations

- "Rockstar," featuring 21 Savage
- "Psycho," featuring Ty Dolla Sign
- "Ball for Me," featuring Nicki Minaj
- "Sunflower," with Swae Lee
- "Spoil My Night," featuring Swae Lee
- "Same Bitches," featuring G-Eazy and YG

Post Malone collaborated with Nicki Minaj on "Ball for Me."

Post Malone

Scan here to listen to Post Malone's "Sunflower" with Swae Law (Official Music Video).

Mixtapes

While you might think of a mixtape as a set of your favorite songs on a playlist you burned to a CD or DVD, in the music business though, it refers to rough cuts of various songs an artist has in the works. The songs on a mixtape may or may not end up on a future album. They show fans that an artist has entered the studio and started working on songs.

Mixtapes often feature numerous collaborations. Record companies encourage their artists to work with other songwriters and producers. This process develops them as songwriters and helps produce a larger body of work than an individual songwriter would create alone. All of the songs an artist writes contribute to their catalog.

AUGUST 26TH
(Released May 12, 2016)

The mixtape's title, "August 26," referred to the intended release date of *Stoney*, his first album. The album got delayed and did not hit stores until December 9, 2016. Malone blamed himself for the delay, saying he and his production team had run into several problems. Although samples are popular in hip-hop, the entire mixtape featured only one, a sample of the Fleetwood Mac hit "Dreams," used on *Hollywood Dreams/Come Down*.

Collaborations

- "Never Understand," featuring Larry June
- "God Damn," featuring 1st
- "Monte," featuring Lil Yachty
- "Lonely," featuring Jaden Smith & Teo

Other Collaborations

- "Burning Man," Watt, from *xXx: Return of Xander Cage*, 2017
- "The Meaning," FKi 1st, John Rawl, JMP, 2016
- "Homemade Dynamite (Remix)," Lorde, also featuring Khalid and SZA, *Melodrama*, 2017
- "You," Dynamite Dylan, *You EP*, 2018
- "Jackie Chan," Tiësto and Dzeko also featuring Preme, non-album single, 2018
- "Notice Me," Migos, *Culture II*, 2018

Scan here to listen to Post Malone's "Lonely" featuring Jaden Smith and Téo.

Post Malone is not just a singer, rapper, and composer—he is also an accomplished musician.

Post Malone

Scan here to listen to "Candy Paint."

Post Malone was honored to work with Kanye West on "Fade."

The Inside Skinny on Some Major Collaborations

Post Malone admitted to being awed by working with Kanye West, referring to the collaboration process as "almost horrifying." He explained he's just nervous going on stage or working with big names in the studio. Malone is a humble guy who enjoys the opportunity to collaborate though.

"FADE" by Kanye West featuring Post Malone
(September 20, 2016)

"I'll tell you what. [Kanye's] got this pad of paper with just like thousands of ideas in it, lines that he'll use. Throughout the day, he'll probably

just think of something and write it down. He flips through and comes up with the craziest stuff, off a freestyle, off a flow." – Malone on working with Kanye West, as told to DJ Whoo Kid.

"PSYCHO AND CANDY PAINT" by Post Malone produced by Louis Bell
(April 27, 2018)

The tracks "Psycho" or "Candy Paint" are good examples of Post getting the beats and vibe together at home in Fruity Loops. He'll send me the basic elements, and I ask myself, "How can I make his vision sound as clear as possible, and what musical elements can I add to develop it? How do I get the best song out of it?" "That's a really fun process. I know that if I'm feeling something, he's going to feel it, because we have a very similar musical barometer for what we like, and similarly eclectic tastes. It's a big advantage when you're not dealing with competing visions for a project where you can get stuck in a cycle of compromising, and no one's really enjoying it. Happily, that's not the case with us." – Producer Louis Bell

Post Malone has a great relationship with his producer Louis Bell.

Watch Keith Urban and Post Malone perform "Baby, What You Want Me To Do" for the Elvis Comeback Special.

THE 50TH ANNIVERSARY OF THE ELVIS COMEBACK SPECIAL
(Broadcast 2019)

"We collaborated on a song that's for an Elvis special coming out in January. I had a blast. He's the real deal. That's what I like about him. He's the real deal. He's just so eclectic, so steeped in all kinds of music. I love him." – Keith Urban

TOURS COMPLETED

Post Malone has completed five major tours of his own as a headliner. He has also toured as a supporting act for other artists, including Alicia Keys on her *Diary* Tour.

OPENING ACT, JUSTIN BIEBER'S PURPOSE TOUR

In March 2016, Justin Bieber announced that he'd handpicked Malone as his opening act for the *Purpose* tour, which spanned the globe. The massive tour stretched into mid-2017 and was supposed to continue into late 2017. Bieber cancelled the remainder of the tour on July 24, 2017. The dates Malone did open for Bieber gave him experience in front of millions of fans and on stage in front of a world audience.

Justin Bieber invited Post Malone to be the opening act for his "*Purpose*" tour which started in 2016.

Scan to listen to Post Malone's single "Wow."

THE *STONEY* TOUR

Malone hit the road on his own for club dates in 2017 after the Bieber tour ended abruptly. He played small club dates in North America, including The Electric Factory in Philadelphia, Pennsylvania, and the House of Blues in Boston, Massachusetts, in September.

THE *POST MALONE* TOUR

The artist's 2019 tour in support of second studio release, *Beerbongs and Bentleys,* traversed the globe with dates in the United Kingdom, North America, and continental Europe. It also included his appearance in the inaugural Super Bowl Music Fest.

Post Malone at the Music Midtown festival in 2018.

Post Malone gained a good deal of experience opening for Justin Bieber by playing to very large crowds.

Blue-eyed soul: The name given to soul music performed by white singers in 1950s and 1960s.

Cultural expropriation: The misappropriation of any culture by another, especially for the purpose of monetary gain or exploitation.

Improvise: In music and acting, a process of making it up as you go along. In music, the artist may generate lyrics in their head and sing them immediately. In rap, this is referred to as "free-styling."

Post Malone at the AMA Awards 2018.

Chapter 2

The Road to the Top—
Fulfilling a Lifelong Dream

Family Life

You would hardly consider Austin Richard Post, better known as Post Malone, to be an All-American boy, but with a birthday of July 4, 1995, the singer exudes natural apple pie vibes. Malone was born and reared in Syracuse, New York, until he was nine years old. He spent the next few years in Grapevine, Texas, near the megacity of Dallas, after his parents moved the family there.

He began playing *Guitar Hero* before he played guitar. In fact, Malone decided to learn to play the real instrument because he so enjoyed the game. When he was ten, his parents gave him a guitar, and he began teaching himself to play.

Post Malone learned to play the guitar as a child. He is now an accomplished guitarist.

SoundCloud — Established in 2007 in Berlin, Germany, SoundCloud is a music-sharing website. It was founded by Swedish sound designer Alexander Ljung and Swedish musician Eric Wahlforss. The platform was intended to help musicians to collaborate by sharing recordings of their work. However, SoundCloud became so successful that it soon became a full-fledged tool for music distribution and challenged other platforms such as MySpace in popularity. By 2010, SoundCloud announced that it had one million users, an incredible feat in such a short period of time. Its success continued, and in 2011 SoundCloud won the Schroders Innovation Award at the European Tech Tour Awards Dinner.

Today, the streaming giant has at least 175 million registered users. SoundCloud also offers two subscription-based services. SoundCloud Pro offers services for musicians, allowing users to upload work. SoundCloud Go, launched in 2016, is a music-streaming service providing an experience free from advertising. Its aim is to compete with Spotify, Apple Music, and similar services. SoundCloud also offers two mobile apps. The main SoundCloud app is for streaming, music discovery, playlists, and sharing. SoundCloud Pulse is for content creators.

As SoundCloud has evolved over the years, it has been criticized for expanding its user base at the expense of the grassroots musicians who were the first to use it. However, with the considerable number of users who are currently registered, it has become a significant music-streaming organization.

Discovery

Malone launched his hip-hop career when he released his debut single, "White Iverson," on SoundCloud in 2015. While it may seem like an out-of-the-blue thing that an artist posted a song there and it became a Billboard Top 20 hit, there is more to it than that.

The rapper left his parents' Texas home after graduating from Grapevine High School and dropping out of college after only a few months. He briefly attended Tarrant County College before leaving to move to Los Angeles with his close friend, Jason Stokes. The two lived

SoundCloud is a music and podcast streaming platform that allows you to listen to millions of songs from around the world, or upload your own.

Scan here to watch as Nicki Swift narrates the Untold Story of Post Malone.

with the gaming band TeamCrafted, who has a popular YouTube channel.

Malone knew he needed to get into the recording studio and asked around about where he should record. A friend recommended Stevie B.'s studio. At the studio, he met 1st and made other music contacts. In fact, 1st created the beat for the single "White Iverson." Rather than **improvise** the lyrics, Malone returned to his home with the beat laid down. He wrote the lyrics over it, then returned to the studio two days later to complete the track.

So, when it hit SoundCloud, the track already had massive internal hip-hop support from the contacts he had made at Stevie B.'s. Luminaries like Wiz Khalifa tweeted about the song, linking to it. The rest is, as they say, history. The massive social media effort spawned a massive fan response and caused the self-published song to peak at the fourteenth spot on the U.S. Billboard Hot 100. Eventually, the song was certified U.S. quadruple platinum. It was the success of the independent recording supported by the collaborative efforts of experienced beat masters and rappers that drew the interest of Republic Records, who signed the part-Jewish, white rapper from Texas to a hip-hop recording contract.

Post Malone at the Baltic Weekend festival in Estonia in 2018.

Post Malone at the 2017 BET Awards. As well as his music, he is also interested in its production.

Post Malone and Self-Education

While Malone did drop out of college, he has continued his self-education. The hip-hop artist remains constantly in the studio and studies the work of others, especially producers like West. He continues to work on his guitar skills and his own production and sound engineering skills.

He also keeps abreast of politics, although he feels that at this time, Americans' votes do not count. He takes staunch stances on political issues, such as gun ownership.

Growing Up in a Non-Musical Family

While his parents did purchase his first guitar, neither is musical themselves. Malone says his dad is his biggest fan, while his mom does not really get his music. Asked once whether he got his dad into his music, he replied that it was the other way around. It is Malone's dad who loves rock music and turned him on to it. His father also got him interested in rap, giving his son "Lean Back" to check out.

In high school, he played in a heavy metal band. Although he also loves country music, especially Hank Williams and George Straight, he did not play any while living in Texas. He plans to cut some now though. In fact, he and Keith Urban collaborated in late 2018 on a song for an Elvis Presley tribute that aired on broadcast television in January 2019.

You might have picked up on his love for basketball from the cultural reference in his first hit, "White Iverson." He enjoys playing and watching the sport, although he admits he is not that good at it.

Becoming a Solo Artist

Although he launched himself as a hip-hop artist, Malone listens to every type of music and does not want to limit himself

Post Malone collaborated with Keith Urban on an Elvis Presley tribute.

Ice-T performing with his heavy metal band Bodycount at the Rock im Park festival in 2018 in Nuremberg, Germany.

to a single genre. Some media outlets have complained that this seems fake of him, expecting a hip-hop artist to remain a hip-hop artist. It is compounded by the fact that he is white. However, the media did the same thing to black artists who chose to cross genres, including rapper/actor Ice T, when he launched his heavy metal band, Bodycount, and Lil Wayne's guitar work. As diverse a catalog as Andre 3000 creates, fans and the media do him the disservice of asking when he'll rap again.

Malone knows from watching his heroes that he'll have a tough time diversifying his catalog and crossing genres. His parody look of '80s and '90s rappers went over surprisingly well. Despite his odd juxtaposition of a fake gold grill and the tats of Nikki Sixx, he has already worked with one of the leading artists known for pushing barriers, mixing genres, creating unique beats, and sampling from a diverse selection of songs—Kanye West.

He likened working with West to working with "Jesus Christ." He was in awe of West's genius and openly shared this with everyone from English interviewers to the director of the Grammy Museum.

His early collaborations could lead to a quick diversification. The opportunities began to arise from his beginnings in Los Angeles while he slept on the floor in a friend's closet. He worked using Fruity Loops to put together rough cuts and played early mixes for any producer who would listen. It worked quickly to get him attention from major names, including one of the biggest in not hip-hop, but white pop Justin Bieber.

He and Bieber collaborated on a single, then another. Bieber chose Malone as his touring partner on the *Purpose* tour. The two also developed a close friendship despite many differences. Bieber hails from Canada and focused his early music career on the

Post Malone is a huge admirer of Kanye West and was delighted to work with him.

Disney set. Long touted as the clean-cut, squeaky-clean choice of moms, he and Malone make an odd couple of best friends. Malone's rock and metal roots gave way to beats and free-style raps.

Becoming Post Malone

Malone says he does not feel weird about being white and rapping because he is an artist who is not defined by his skin color. He also does not plan to only rap, following in the footsteps of those before him. Since he was ten, he has wanted to perform country music and now plans to do so. He also enjoys pop and rock though.

Although it may seem odd for a part-Jewish guy to rap, there is a precedent and not just the Beastie Boys. Historically, white performers have created covers of black performers' songs or written original music in the same genre in order to help it reach a larger audience. This occurred en masse in the 1950s and 1960s with soul and **blue-eyed soul**.

Black artists merged the genres of gospel music with rhythm and blues and jazz, performing it in jazz clubs throughout the U.S. It was an original kind of music that expressed hope, love, and passion. It also was illegal for black artists to perform in white nightclubs at the time or for whites to attend shows or even enter black establishments, due to a set of laws that enforced segregation.

In this manner, white artists helped share a cultural phenomenon and break barriers. Rather than **cultural expropriation**, they helped popularize the music. It was within music and sports that the barriers of segregation were first broken, with artists and athletes of differing races openly choosing to work together. Although many things have changed in the early 21st century, Malone does help the rap community to reach a larger audience that it normally would not, and vice versa.

He also feels there's more to life than music. He's branched out as an entrepreneur, and *Forbes* magazine, a bastion of fiscal news, calls him the musical Donald Trump. Poor Malone. He's not a Trump supporter, but he can surprisingly finesse an audience when in the right frame of mind, and his in-depth interviews reveal this.

He's also moving into life as an actor. Since moving to California in 2015, he's guested in a number of other artists' videos. It whetted his appetite, and he's now landed his first acting role and completed his first voiceover role.

The Beastie Boys is another act that made a success of a genre usually performed by black artists.

Post Malone does not just define himself as a rap artist, he has ideas for other projects in the future, including being a country singer.

Post Malone
HIP-HOP & R&B

Text-Dependent Questions:

1. What kind of musical group did Post Malone perform with in high school?

2. What parts of Malone's act or schtick are parody?

3. Why are collaborations between artists like Post Malone and Kanye West so important? What is their historical significance to music and to culture?

Research Project:

Malone continues the tradition of blue-eyed soul in hip-hop. Research the original soul performers such as Aretha Franklin, Ray Charles, and Otis Redding, and blue-eyed soul performers such as the Bee Gees, Dusty Springfield, and The Righteous Brothers. Choose one song that both a soul artist and a blue-eyed soul artist recorded, and compare and contrast the performance style and production. What do they have in common? What do they do differently? This applies musically and in their pronunciations and delivery.

Caricature: An exaggerated imitation of, or a rendered image of, a person, showing comedically distorted features of the subject and oversimplification of their personality, such as in film, literature, or theater.

Film short: A documentary or narrative film running 40 minutes or less.

Voiceover: In a broadcast or film, when a voice that is not the narrator speaks dialogue over synchronous action. This is how animated characters are voiced.

Post Malone at Michigan Lottery Amphitheatre at Freedom Hill in 2018.

Chapter 3

Post Malone's Hip-Hop Career, Interests, and Passions in Moments

More Than Just a Rapper

Upon achieving success as a hip-hop artist, Post Malone claimed he's not one, but an artist. If the line seems unclear, it is because he is thinking in terms of a long-term career that spans genres. He's had designs on being a country musician since childhood. He played heavy metal while a teen. He's secretly hiding a talent for crooning blue-eyed soul. He's also confounded most music critics who simply have not recognized the friendly parody with which he began his career. Instead, critics took him seriously and got offended by his caricature, while the artists at the top of the hip-hop charts embraced his native talent and sense of humor.

Ultimately, Post Malone is praised for his talent whatever the genre.

Malone told an interviewer in Poland that he chose to start with hip-hop "because it's fun. I think hip-hop is important because it brings people together in a beautiful, happy way. Everybody's happy."

He looks to folk musicians like Bob Dylan to make him cry. Yet, he keeps moving toward folk and country. There's no harm in exploring genres, something many artists do over time. Malone simply planned from the start, which for him was the age of 16, making mixtapes in his Texas hometown. For Malone, whose early musical influences included country, rap and rock, it's a normal development.

So is contributing to film soundtracks, which he's already done a handful of times. He's also getting involved in film in another manner—as an actor.

The Life of an Actor

Post Malone enjoys comedy skits and sketch work. He built an entire musical persona as a joke. He could cover the blue-eyed soul artist Robin Gibb's "I Started a Joke" to see how many fans get it. Although he lost the fake gold grill he sported during the release of his first studio release, he continues to record hip-hop and rap. Plus, he's moved beyond the comedy skits he shot to promote the Omaze giveaway (a charitable cause), to filming a part in the Netflix movie *Wonderland*.

Wonderland wraps in 2019 and stars Mark Wahlberg as Spenser, the reformed felon from the Robert B. Parker mystery novels that were adapted for television in the 1980s as *Spenser for Hire*. Malone's part in the film represents his first foray into feature film.

In 2018, he worked as a **voiceover** artist on the animation project *Spider-Man: Into the Spider-Verse*. He voiced a small part, "Brooklyn Bystander." He also contributed a song to its soundtrack, making it his fifth soundtrack credit. Until recently, his Internet Movie Database credits included a number of **film shorts** – music videos in which he'd appeared.

Helping Others Get Their Start

Amidst this flurry of activity, he re-entered the studio in June of 2018 to work on songs for his third studio album. He continues to work in the same studios with some of the same friends who came out to California with him from Texas. Those fellow musicians already had some production experience but had not yet "made it." Malone continues to work with them on each of his tracks and to garner them introductions to the same bigwigs he meets.

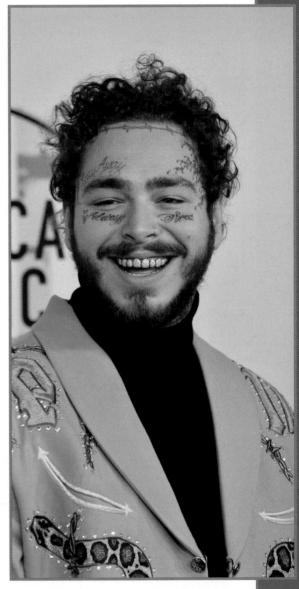

Post Malone has branched out into voiceovers and small acting parts.

Endorsements

CROCS

Another Post Malone collaboration addresses fashion. He's a guest designer for Crocs. He's worked with the brand twice, churning out limited-edition styles for them. His first design sold out in ten minutes.

His Crocs Dimitri clog moved so quickly that the casual shoe brand decided to partner with him on a second style. The designers are a part of the brand's second year of the Come As You Are Campaign, celebrating individual uniqueness and the comfort of self-confidence.

"I wear Crocs everywhere from the bar to the stage, and I felt it was the perfect collaboration to get together with Crocs and give the fans what they've been asking for," Malone said in an interview.

The Dimitri clog comes in white only and features a baby devil face motif, a "Posty Co." label on its

The above image does not represent a Post Malone product.

Scan here to watch an interview with Post Malone where he says working with Kanye West was "almost horrifying," how he loves folk music and working with fellow musicians and producers from Dallas, TX.

Voicing Animated Films—Voice actors provide the voices for animated characters, acting out the script in a sound booth while an audio engineer records their words. Multiple actors work together at one time, acting out the scenes, each speaking into their own microphone. For some parts, an actor will read their lines alone, making it more challenging, since they have no one else to play off of. To break into this area, you need a booming voice or a cute sound that sets your voice apart. Once recorded, the audio files are merged with the animated sequences using a computer program to sync the files by timecode.

heel and six original Jibbitz charms, among them an eyeball, barbed wire, and the rapper's "Stay Away" tattoo.

His second design drew inspiration from his sophomore release, *Beerbongs & Bentleys*. It comes only in yellow and uses the Classic Clog shape. Malone added a black barbed wire motif and another six charms.

Both pairs retail for $59.99. The first pair was available only through the Crocs website, but the second design also hit stores in Malone's home states of New York and Texas, as well as California and Florida.

Luc Belaire

Post Malone also represents the French winemaking brand Luc Belaire. Established in

continued on page 46

Awards Won

Post Malone opened his budding career as a musician with a few big wins in 2018. While his chart toppers have yet to take firm hold with critics, fans have ensured that his singles and album releases continue to break chart and sales records. Malone has set a goal of a Grammy win for himself.

American Music Awards

Favorite Male Artist – Pop/Rock | Won in 2018
Favorite Rap/Hip-Hop Album – Pop/Rock | Won in 2018

Billboard Awards

Top Rap Song, "Rockstar," featuring 21 Savage | Won in 2018

MTV Video Music Awards

Song of the Year, "Rockstar," featuring 21 Savage | Won in 2018

Nominations

In a relatively short career, Post Malone has received many nominations for awards.

American Music Awards

New Artist of the Year | Nominated in 2017

Artist of the Year | Nominated in 2018

Collaboration of the Year with Savage 21 – "Rockstar" | Nominated in 2018

Favorite Artist Rap/Hip-Hop | Nominated in 2018

Favorite Song Rap/Hip-Hop – "Rockstar" | Nominated in 2018

ARIA Awards

Best International Artist – *Beerbongs & Bentleys and Stoney* | Nominated in 2018

BET Hip-Hop Awards

Best Collaboration, Duo or Group – "Rockstar" | Nominated in 2018

Billboard Music Awards

Top Collaboration "Rockstar," featuring Savage 21 | Nominated in 2018

Top Streaming Song (Audio) "Congratulations," featuring Quavo | Nominated in 2018

Top Streaming Song (Audio) "Rockstar," featuring Savage 21 | Nominated in 2018

Top Hot 100 Song "Rockstar," featuring Savage 21 | Nominated in 2018

Top Rap Album *Stoney* | Nominated in 2018

Top Billboard 200 Album *Stoney* | Nominated in 2018

Top Rap Male Artist *Stoney* | Nominated in 2018
Top Rap Artist *Stoney* | Nominated in 2018
Top Streaming Songs Artist *Stoney* | Nominated in 2018
Top Hot 100 Artist *Stoney* | Nominated in 2018
Top Male Artist *Stoney* | Nominated in 2018

Grammy Awards

Record "Rockstar," 21 Savage, Louis Bell, Tank God, Manny Marroquin, Mike Bozzi | Nominated in 2019
Album *Beerbongs & Bentleys* Louis Bell, Manny Marroquin, Austin Post, Mike Bozzi | Nominated in 2019
Best Pop Solo Performance "Better Now" | Nominated in 2019
Best Rap/Sung Performance "Rockstar," featuring Savage 21 | Nominated in 2019

MTV Video Music Awards

Artist | Nominated in 2018

People's Choice Awards

Male Artist | Nominated in 2018
Song "Psycho," featuring y Dolla $ign | Nominated in 2018
Album *Beerbongs & Bentleys* | Nominated in 2018
Music Video "Psycho," featuring y Dolla $ign | Nominated in 2018

Post Malone with two awards won at the AMAs in 2018. The awards were for Favorite Hip-Hop/Rap Album and Favorite Male Artist.

Scan here to watch Post Malone in conversation with Brett Berish, CEO of Luc Belaire, about his success as part of the "Self Made Tastes Better" campaign.

1898, the Maison has created a selection of wines for six generations. Known for its "elegant, refreshing blend," the venerable brand partnered with Malone for its "Self-Made Tastes Better" campaign. The vintner created an interview show to feature each of the influencers with which it partnered. Malone serves as the guest in the first episode of season one. Other interviewees in season one include Rick Ross and DJ Khaled.

Success Doesn't Happen Overnight

Determined, hardworking, and relentless describe the traits leading to Malone's success. While the artist exhibits a very laid-back demeanor, he also commits to a dedicated work ethic. Many musicians cause fans to wait years between projects, but Malone, despite being late with one project by a few months, continually works. Only six weeks after his second studio release was released, the rapper had re-entered the studio to record new songs while planning his world tour in support of *Beerbongs and Bentleys.* Malone consistently looks for new projects that move his career in different directions, whether it is recording in a new genre of music or voicing an animated character or acting on screen or designing shoes. Post Malone determined that he wanted to make it. Once he made it, he is set on staying at the top.

Text-Dependent Questions:

1. On what project did Malone contribute both acting and music skills?

2. What side career has Malone started for one of his endorsements?

3. What goal has Malone set for himself in music?

Research Project:

Post Malone has segued from contributing songs to other artists' CDs to contributing songs to film soundtracks. Research how film soundtracks are created. Who selects the music? How are the music selections fit to the film?

Cross-genre: In music, a song or album that draws from more than one genre to cross chart lines. For example, a country-rock song or a pop-metal song.

Disrupter: In business, any product or service that produces radical change to the industry or business strategy through the introduction of a new product or service that results in the creation of a new market.

Signature: A person's or brand's trademark or hallmark by which they are immediately recognizable.

Post Malone is a self-made millionaire earned through talent and dedication.

Chapter 4

Post Malone's Brand Messaging—Becoming a Worldwide Sensation

Post Malone's Marketing Strategy

In business, there's a higher modicum of respect for self-made success. Following the success of Post Malone's sophomore studio effort, he boasts a net worth of about $8 million. Not shabby for a guy who once slept in his friend's closet.

The rapper says that being self-made means creating success without cutting corners or changing yourself to impress the masses. Staying true to oneself means ignoring the hate people dump on you and when they doubt you. It is about knowing when to listen to advice about how to do things, and when to ignore it.

As Malone shows, the Internet has provided the shift in business to make self-made individuals an actual, attainable business model. He is one of the first of a new generation to abandon a traditional

Post Malone's hard work is paying off, with awards won in 2018 for his first album *Stoney*.

career path and the traditional method of achieving success in his chosen field. Instead, he became an industry **disrupter** who leveraged developing technologies to forge ahead creatively. The artist chose SoundCloud as his operations base, then used social media, including Facebook, Instagram, Twitter, and YouTube as his influence engines. He networked with the contacts he'd made at Stevie B.'s studio and gained help from them to publicize his initial single on social media. With Wiz Khalifa as an influencer, among others, Malone was able to reach a massive audience of interested, engaged customers easily.

Scan here to watch Nessa interview Post Malone. He speaks about working with Kanye West and making country music.

Collaboration Creates Opportunity

His collaborations with successful hip-hop artists guaranteed an already interested fan base that gained him even more fans and publicity. This led to many producers wanting to work with him on his new music. His concerted efforts resulted in more than 100 million streams for "White Iverson" on self-publishing music site SoundCloud and about 400 million YouTube views. It was more than enough to get him signed. He vaulted his sophomore effort into a platinum album and his first Top 10 hit.

Post Malone performing at the Rock Werchter Festival in Belgium in 2018.

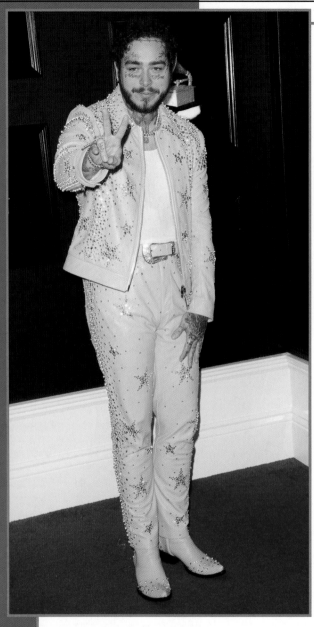

Post Malone at the 61st Grammy Awards at the Staples Center in 2019 in Los Angeles.

For millennials, Malone's **cross-genre** and cross-disciplinary projects and partnerships in other industries simply reflect a more well-rounded scope and vision.

"It was surreal to see so many people I looked up to and respect showing so much love. I was still so new to everything, and these are people who've been killing it for a long time. It's really important that the people I look up to love the music," he told one interviewer.

For millennials, Malone's cross-disciplinary projects and partnerships in other industries simply reflect a more well-rounded scope and vision. For him, the need is more than creating, but in doing it his own way.

"If someone tells you no, being self-made is having the ability to tell them to shut up, and you keep rocking anyway.

It's being able to get it done your own way. People are going to hate on you, doubt you, and tell you how you should do things—you have to stay true to yourself and do things on your own terms," Malone said.

Rather than cave to pressure to be someone he's not, Malone calls it "super important" to be yourself.

"If you're being yourself, and it's dope, people are going to rock with you and create trends out of what you do."

He says he went through a phase where he wanted to be just like A$AP Rocky. He got over it and developed his own **signature** style and sound.

"I realized that I'm cool, too. I can make waves with my own sound and my own style. That's when I stopped fearing what everybody thought and started doing what I wanted to do, and what I thought was dope."

Seeing people he respected in the business respond favorably to his work made him more confident. Malone counsels people who want to follow in his footsteps to create success to do something original and not follow trends.

"Rock with yourself, and you'll make something sick. Trust yourself and your process. You have to do things on your own time that feel right to you," the artist explained in an interview with Luc Belaire.

Scan here to watch Post Malone guest star on Martha Stewart's and Snoop Dogg's "Potluck Dinner Party."

Youth Entrepreneurship—Future Business Leaders of America (FBLA) The FBLA provides junior high school and high school students training to become community-minded business leaders. It provides career preparation, leadership development, academic competitions, and educational programs. Students hold officer positions in their local chapters and at state and national levels. They develop transferable skills while attending seminars and workshops. They compete in academic contests by building a local business with other students that generates a product and sells it. The businesses compete based on sales and other data. The program also teaches community service by having its members partner with the March of Dimes to fundraise and build awareness.

One key to success for Malone has been finding a motivation that keeps him going. He had to find something that made him want to keep creating and to continually push the bounds of what he'd already achieved.

Shutting down haters became a motivation for him. So did making something great for his fans. Malone set a goal of winning a Grammy.

"I want to show people I'm not a one-hit wonder, or some kind of overnight success story. I want people to know I'm going to be here for a minute, and if you don't like it — there's nothing you can do about it," he said in 2018.

His daily goal is simple: make the best music he can. He's focused on creating "truly unique" works while collaborating with some of the best artists the music industry has to offer.

Post Malone was nominated for four Grammys in 2019, including two for "Rockstar," one for "Better Now," and one for the album *Beerbongs & Bentleys*.

Post Malone is interested in fashion. He wore this flamboyant suit at the American Music Awards.

Diversify and Expand

Malone also does not want to limit himself to the music business. He wants to combine his music with fashion and lifestyle brands. The artist recognizes that the artist represents the art.

"You are what your music represents.... Bring something fresh and unique to the game that will make people remember you. That will force people to listen to you, then from there, they will get to know who you are and what you care about."

He observed that in today's music industry it boils down to 50 percent music and 50 percent who you are—your personality. Social media helps people share themselves. Rather than creating cookie cutters, it requires uniqueness.

"All of the legends are dope and killing it, "Malone

Fast Fact 4:

Self-Publishing—In book or music publishing, *self-publishing* refers to the author publishing the media without involving an established publisher such as a record company or book publisher. In music, the platforms of Garage Band, iTunes, and SoundCloud are used for self-publishing. These mechanisms let the artist control the contents and release data, publicity, and payments. Rather than receiving royalty payments on their own work from a record company, the artist receives direct payment from the fan upon purchase of an album or song.

explained to Berish. "From fashion to the way they act, every legend has their own thing that they're known for."

Success means following your gut and standing up for yourself.

"I've just realized that I have to follow what I think is best because, at the end of the day, it's my life and career," the artist said.

Malone says that today's entrepreneurial focus and business independence let society "celebrate individuality and all the different people paving their own way." He says people need to feel like they can find success on their own.

Persevere

Since he is just 23, it may seem that he experienced an overnight success. Actually, to become a success in hip-hop as a young white man from Texas required perseverance. He began creating mixtapes at the age of 16. He moved to Los Angeles at the age of 18. That meant four years of believing in himself while living in less-than-ideal conditions. It required daily hard work and effort. Creating hit music requires a commitment to a daily schedule and work week, just like building a building would.

He showed up at the studio, ready to work every day. He networked, meeting everyone he could and asking one studio connection to introduce him to another.

Collaborating helped put him in the right crowd to help promote his music. Being himself and being a likable person whom others could respect made them want to help him.

Post Malone uses social media to promote his work and to keep in touch with his fans, even when he is really busy.

While people may see an "overnight sensation," in reality, they're seeing the product of 13 years of work. They're seeing Malone, so determined to learn to play guitar, that at ten years old he was watching YouTube videos to learn chords and chord choices. Today's success actually began 13 years ago with a determined little boy who wanted to learn to play and perform music.

Social Media Tactics

Post Malone actively uses every major social media platform. He has taken a break from social media in the past, though, after being verbally attacked on Twitter. He's continued posting, though, throughout personal crises and his busy production schedules.

Branding the Name Post Malone

Malone stands as a testament to embracing authenticity and a sense of humor in your branding. As some fans point out, he's hard not to like, since the artist, as one fan described it, "doesn't have a mean bone in his body." Perhaps that's part of his uniqueness. In the hip-hop industry, most performers still tout their former gang affiliation. Tough is the name of the game. Its performers, especially the old school, hail from zip codes in Compton or Watts, not Grapevine, TX.

Post Malone truly embraces the branding tenet of authenticity wholly. His honesty is his weapon.

Post Malone is a global phenomenon. He has performed in Europe to a large European fan base.

Post Malone
HIP-HOP & R&B

Text-Dependent Questions:

① Think of a business product you and your classmates could create and market through a program like FBLA. How would you get local support, including manufacturing, if needed?

② Where does Malone find his motivations?

③ How does Malone advise others to develop their personal brand?

Research Project:

Research joining your local FBLA chapter. If there is none, find out how you could start one to jumpstart the entrepreneurial efforts and education of you and your schoolmates.

Words to Understand

Audio engineering: In music, the audio engineer handles the technical aspects of a sound recording and works with a record producer or director. In smaller projects, the same person may do the job of sound engineer and producer.

Feminist: A person who advocates for women's rights based upon equality of genders.

Skit: A short, informal scene that informs or entertains through a theater performance.

Post Malone supports Folds of Honor which provides help for the families of injured or fallen veterans.

Charitable Work: Giving Back to the Community

Post Malone has only been in the music business for five years professionally, but he has already developed a platform of philanthropical issues that are important to him. His early charity work has included support for the families of deceased and disabled military veterans, Alzheimer's disease research, and gender equality.

Folds of Honor

In partnership with Omaze, Malone donated a Bentley automobile for a fundraising raffle to benefit the Folds of Honor charity. Founded in 2007, the Folds of Honor provides educational scholarships to the children and spouses of deceased and disabled U.S. military service members. Fans donated to the charity in amounts of $5 to

Research to find a cure for Alzheimer's disease is a cause close to Post Malone's heart.

Deaths at War–While Folds of Honor focuses on helping the survivors of U.S. troops who perish in battle, loss of life in war is a global issue. War and Peace tracks battle-related deaths in state or national conflicts worldwide. Its statistics go back to 1946. Although the number of people who die during wartime has decreased since 1946, the number remains significant. War and Peace's statistics track deaths in battles where more than 25 battle-related deaths occurred. During the initial year of statistical tracking, 1946, globally, 295,541 soldiers lost their lives in battle. In 2016, the most recent for complete statistics, 87,432 soldiers lost their lives in battle. The year of the greatest loss of life was 1950, when 546,501 soldiers perished in battle.

$5,000 to purchase contest entries. The Bentley winner also received a first cruise in the car with Post Malone.

Malone disguised himself as a record store clerk to promote the giveaway. He spent the day in a uniform, wearing glasses and discussing music with customers, the majority of whom listened to classical or pop. With cameras rolling behind the scenes, he pitched his music to the unwitting public. He only got recognized twice, but the **skits** made the perfect comedy to promote the fundraiser with Omaze.

Hilarity for Charity

Comedian Seth Rogen's Hilarity for Charity event encompassed music, comedy sketches, and stand-up comedy to raise research funds for, and awareness of, Alzheimer's disease. The event directly benefited The Alzheimer's Association, the leading voluntary health organization for Alzheimer's care, support, and research. Post Malone

performed the soulful, romantic ballad "Return of the Mack," originally performed by Mark Morrison. While his intent may have been a send-up or parody, the performance revealed his mellow singing voice to the audience. In the wake of the broadcast performance, the Internet lit up with comments from surprised 30- and 40-somethings who had not previously listened to his music. His cover of the 1996 break-up song impressed them enough to check out his other music, according to their comments on a variety of music forums.

Post Malone donated a Bentley to a fundraiser in support of the Folds of Honor charity.

Post Malone actively encourages women to seek careers in the male-dominated world of audio engineering.

Post Malone
HIP-HOP & R&B

Alzheimer's disease — The term *Alzheimer's disease* refers to a type of dementia that creates behavior, memory, and thinking issues. Its symptoms generally develop slowly and worsen over time, eventually eroding the ability of the individual to carry on conversation or respond to environmental cues. They eventually become so severe as to interfere with everyday life and tasks. This cognitive disease accounts for between 60 and 80 percent of dementia cases but is not considered a normal part of aging. While the majority of those diagnosed with Alzheimer's are aged 65 or older, another type, early-onset Alzheimer's, affects those younger than 65. In the U.S. alone, about 200,000 people have a diagnosis of early-onset Alzheimer's. It is the sixth leading cause of death in the U.S.

Pro-Diversity and Gender Equality

In 2019, Post Malone joined a gender equality campaign founded by the Recording Academy that focuses on employing more females in audio engineering, producing, and mixing roles. Currently, females comprise

Post Malone is a strong believer in gender equality and actively encourages females to work in male-dominated industries.

only three percent of the individuals employed in such roles in the music industry. Malone joins 200 other stakeholders, including other artists and producers and record labels. His friend Justin Bieber and prior collaborators Nicki Minaj and Keith Urban also joined the **feminist** initiative.

How Post Malone Reminds Us to Give Back

Post Malone reaches out to his fans through social media, providing information on charities of interest to him. He promotes events and fundraisers and encourages his fans to give of themselves. He makes live appearances and sings and acts in productions that fundraise.

Post Malone has used his creativity to enhance the lives of others. Today, he continues to inspire and encourage all his fans to follow their dreams.

Text-Dependent Questions:

1. How could you plan a local version of Hilarity for Charity?

2. What is one issue of gender equality in music?

3. How many other music industry professionals are involved in the pro-diversity campaign?

Research Project:

Choose a medical issue like Alzheimer's disease, and research how it affects your community. How many people does it affect? What local or regional philanthropies or charities exist to help find a cure or treatments?

Series Glossary of Key Terms

A&R: an abbreviation that stands for Artists and Repertoire, which is a record company department responsible for the recruitment and development of talent; similar to a talent scout for sports.

ambient: a musical style that relies on electronic sounds, gentle music, and the lack of a regular beat to create a relaxed mood for the listener.

brand: a particular product or a characteristic that serves to identify a particular product; a brand name is one having a well-known and usually highly regarded or marketable word or phrase.

cameo: also called a cameo role; a minor part played by a prominent performer in a single scene of a motion picture or a television show.

choreography: the art of planning and arranging the movements, steps, and patterns of dancers.

collaboration: a product created by working with someone else; combining individual talents.

debut: a first public appearance on a stage, on television, or so on, or the beginning of a profession or career; the first appearance of something, like a new product.

deejay (DJ): a slang term for a person who spins vinyl records on a turntable; aka a disc jockey.

demo: a recording of a new song, or of one performed by an unknown singer or group, distributed to disc jockeys, recording companies, and the like, to demonstrate the merits of the song or performer.

dubbed: something that is named or given a new name or title; in movies, when the actors' voices have been replaced with those of different performers speaking another language; in music, transfer or copying of previously recorded audio material from one medium to another.

endorsement: money earned from a product recommendation, typically by a celebrity, athlete, or other public figure.

entrepreneur: a person who organizes and manages any enterprise, especially a business, usually with considerable initiative and at financial risk.

falsetto: a man singing in an unnaturally high voice, accomplished by creating a vibration at the very edge of the vocal chords.

genre: a subgroup or category within a classification, typically associated with works of art, such as music or literature.

hone, honing: sharpening or refining a set of skills necessary to achieve success or perform a specific task.

icon: a symbol that represents something, such as a team, a religious person, a location, or an idea.

innovation: the introduction of something new or different; a brand-new feature or upgrade to an existing idea, method, or item.

instrumental: serving as a crucial means, agent, or tool; of, relating to, or done with an instrument or tool.

jingle: a short verse, tune, or slogan used in advertising to make a product easily remembered.

mogul: someone considered to be very important, powerful, and in charge; a term usually associated with heads of businesses in the television, movie studio, or recording industries.

performing arts: skills that require public performance, as acting, singing, or dancing.

philanthropy: goodwill to fellow members of the human race; an active effort to promote human welfare.

public relations: the activity or job of providing information about a particular person or organization to the public so that people will regard that person or organization in a favorable way.

sampler: a digital or electronic musical instrument, related to a synthesizer, that uses samples, or sound recordings, of real instruments (trumpet, violin, piano, etc.) mixed with excerpts of recorded songs and other interesting sounds (sirens, ocean waves, construction noises, car horns, etc.) that are stored digitally and can be replayed by a triggering device, like a sequencer, electronic drums, or a MIDI keyboard.

single: a music recording having two or more tracks that is shorter than an album, EP, or LP; also, a song that is particularly popular, independent of other songs on the same album or by the same artist.

Further Reading

Cooper, B. Lee and Hoffmann, Frank W. *Blue-Eyed Soul: Myths and Reality In American Popular Music*. CreateSpace Independent Publishing Platform. 2018.

Michael, Haralambos. *Soul Music: The Birth of a Sound in Black America*. Da Capo Press. 1985.

Orlando, Maya. *Post Malone Adult Coloring Book: Millennial Culture Rapper and Trap Legend, Billboards Hot Producer and Epic Artist Inspired Adult Coloring Book*. CreateSpace Independent Publishing Platform. 2018.

Internet Resources

www.billboard.com
The official site of Billboard Music, with articles about artists, chart information, and more.

www.thefader.com/
Official website for a popular New York City–based music magazine.

www.hiphopweekly.com
A young-adult hip-hop magazine.

www.thesource.com/
Website for a bi-monthly magazine that covers hip-hop and pop culture.

https://www.instagram.com/postmalone/
Post Malone's official Instagram for all the latest photos.

https://twitter.com/PostMalone
Post Malone's official Twitter for all the latest news and updates.

https://www.facebook.com/postmalone/
 Post Malone's official Facebook page for all the latest news and updates.

http://www.postmalone.com
Post Malone's official website—the go-to source for all official updates and music.

Citations

McIntyre, Hugh. "Post Malone Sets a New Record for the Most Simultaneous Top 40 Hits." *Forbes*. May 9, 2018. https://www.forbes.com/sites/hughmcintyre/2018/05/09/post-malone-sets-a-new-record-for-the-most-simultaneous-top-40-hits/#1fe115b2d32e

McIntyre, Hugh. "Post Malone's 'Beerbongs & Bentleys' Opens at No. 1 With a Massive First Week." *Forbes*. May 6, 2018. https://www.forbes.com/sites/hughmcintyre/2018/05/06/post-malones-beerbongs-bentleys-opens-at-no-1-with-a-massive-first-week/#33f784e23a96

Malone, Post. "August 26." *DatPiff*. May 12, 2016. https://www.datpiff.com/Post-Malone-August-26th-mixtape.783234.html

"Post Malone." *IMDB*. Accessed February 2, 2019. https://www.imdb.com/name/nm8203589/

"Blue-eyed soul." *Britannica*. Accessed February 3, 2019. https://www.britannica.com/art/blue-eyed-soul

Mitchell, Julian. Forbes. "The Art of Being Self-Made: A Conversation With Post Malone." *Forbes*. August 31, 2017. https://www.forbes.com/sites/julianmitchell/2017/08/31/the-art-of-being-self-made-a-conversation-with-post-malone/#10193f1740f1

Post Malone. *All American Speakers*. Accessed February 2, 2019. https://www.allamericanspeakers.com/speakers/408837/Post-Malone

Setaro, Shawn. "Here's Why Post Malone Is a Problem." *Complex*. November 27, 2017. https://www.complex.com/music/2017/11/post-malone-and-racism

"R&B." *The Soul Music Sanctuary*. Accessed February 4, 2019. http://www.soulmusicsanctuary.net/soul-musics-history.html

"What was the last public school to desegregate in the U.S.? And when?" *Stack Exchange*. Accessed February 4, 2019. https://history.stackexchange.com/questions/10304/what-was-the-last-public-school-to-desegregate-in-the-us-and-when

"Brown v. Board at Fifty: "With an Even Hand" A Century of Racial Segregation, 1849–1950." *The Library of Congress*. Accessed February 4, 2019. https://www.loc.gov/exhibits/brown/brown-segregation.html

Weiss, Jeff. "Post Malone is the perfect pop star for this American moment. That's not a compliment." *The Washington Post*. October 30, 2018 https://www.washingtonpost.com/lifestyle/post-malone-is-the-perfect-pop-star-for-this-american-moment-thats-not-a-compliment/2018/10/30/ad6112b8-dbc4-11e8-b732-3c72cbf131f2_story.html?noredirect=on&utm_term=.ca7db296c522

Keith Urban Collaborates With Post Malone for Elvis TV Special." *Mega Country*. November 28, 2018. http://www.megacountry.com/news/16166-keith-urban-collaborates-with-post-malone-for-elvis-tv-special-033

Parizot, Matthew. "Post Malone Is Already Working on His Next Album." *Hot New Hip Hop*. June 5, 2018.

Schneider-Levy, Barbara. "Post Malone Collaborated With Crocs On a Limited-Edition Style — & It Sold Out in 10 Minutes." *Footwear News*. November 1, 2018. https://footwearnews.com/2018/fashion/collaborations/post-malone-crocs-dimitri-clog-sold-out-1202701977/

Preston, Stefan. "Post Malone's Second Crocs Collaboration With a Barbed Wire Pattern Is Reselling at an Unbelievable Price." *The Cheat Sheet*. December 18, 2018.

Post Malone Clothing & Accessories. *Zumiez*. Accessed February 2, 2019. https://www.zumiez.com/brands/post-malone.html

Wood, Mikael. "Why Post Malone has been called 'the Donald Trump of hip-hop.'" *Los Angeles Times*. December 16, 2016. https://www.latimes.com/entertainment/music/la-et-ms-post-malone-20161216-story.html

Ch, Devin. "Cardi B, Post Malone & Ariana Grande Join Grammy's New Feminist-Initiative." *Hot New Hip Hop*. February 1, 2019. https://www.hotnewhiphop.com/cardi-b-post-malone-and-ariana-grande-join-grammys-new-feminist-initiative-news.70884.html

Post Malone Tour. *Post Malone Tour*. Accessed February 4, 2019. https://www.postmalonetour.com/

Copper, Joshua. "Justin Bieber and Post Malone's Beautiful Bromance: A Timeline." *Spin*. August 20, 2018. https://www.spin.com/2018/08/justin-bieber-post-malone-relationship-timeline/

Roser, Max. "War and Peace." *Our World in Data*. Accessed February 3, 2019. https://ourworldindata.org/war-and-peace

"What Is Alzheimer's?" *Alzheimer's Association*. Accessed February 3, 2019. https://www.alz.org/alzheimers-dementia/what-is-alzheimers

"Post Malone's Crocs and other strange celebrity endorsements." *BBC*. November 3, 2018. https://www.bbc.com/news/newsbeat-46083446

"Post Malone's Crocs and other strange celebrity endorsements." *Popular Newspaper*. November 3, 2018. https://popularnewspaper.com/post-malones-crocs-and-other-strange-celebrity-endorsements/

Roberts, Randall. "Post Malone to team up with Red Hot Chili Peppers at Grammys." *The Columbian*. January 31, 2019. https://www.columbian.com/news/2019/jan/31/post-malone-to-team-up-with-red-hot-chili-peppers-on-grammys/

Mahadevan, Tara. "Post Malone Calls His Music 'So Bad' in Undercover Record Store Prank." *Complex*. October 16, 2018. https://www.complex.com/music/2018/10/post-malone-calls-his-music-so-bad-undercover-record-store-prank

Bell, Brian. "Seth Rogen's Hilarity for Charity Packs Everyone From Post Malone to Tiffany Haddish Into New Trailer." *Paste Magazine*. Accessed February 2, 2019. https://www.pastemagazine.com/articles/2018/04/watch-seth-rogens-hilarity-for-charity-pack-everyo.html

Casteel, Beth. "Post Malone announces charity campaign, goes undercover." *AltPress*. October 16, 2018. https://www.altpress.com/news/post-malone-omaze-campaign-announcement-video-2/

Crawford, Lauren. Post Malone Is Now Designing Crocs & It Actually Makes Total Sense. I Heart Radio. November 1, 2018. https://www.iheart.com/content/2018-11-01-post-malone-is-now-designing-crocs-it-actually-makes-total-sense/

"Self-Made Tastes Better." Luc Belaire. Accessed February 4, 2019. https://www.lucbelaire.com/movement.html

"About FBLA-PBL." *Future Business Leaders of America*. Accessed February 4, 2019. https://www.fbla-pbl.org/about/

Educational Video Links

Chapter 1:

http://x-qr.net/1LLc
http://x-qr.net/1JD0
http://x-qr.net/1Jiq
http://x-qr.net/1L19
http://x-qr.net/1Kmm
http://x-qr.net/1LkT
http://x-qr.net/1J9x
http://x-qr.net/1KCk

Chapter 2:

http://x-qr.net/1KBG

Chapter 3:

http://x-qr.net/1KaZ
http://x-qr.net/1Hyw

Chapter 4:

http://x-qr.net/1Jhq
http://x-qr.net/1KsD
http://x-qr.net/1K2p

Chapter 5:

http://x-qr.net/1M1i
http://x-qr.net/1KGQ

Index

Index

Index

Post Malone HIP-HOP & R&B

Picture Credits

Chapter 1:

Glen Francis www.PacificProDigital.com
Wikimedia Commons
The Come Up Show | Wikimedia Commons
Diego_bf109 | Wikimedia Commons
Tinseltown | Shutterstock.com
Jamie Lamor Thompson | Shutterstock.com
Tinseltown | Shutterstock.com
Kathy Hutchins | Shutterstock.com
Featureflash Photo Agency/Henry Harris |
Shutterstock.com
Janek Sergejev | Shutterstock.com
Tinseltown | Shutterstock.com
The Come Up Show | Wikimedia Commons
Jack Fordyce | Shutterstock.com
Jamie Lamor Thompson | Shutterstock.com

Chapter 2:

Kathy Hutchins | Shutterstock.com
UNIKYLUCKK | Shutterstock.com
Dennizn | Shutterstock.com
Janek Sergejev | Shutterstock.com
Arthuro Holmes | Shutterstock.com
Debby Wong | Shutterstock.com
Milan Risky | Shutterstock.com
S_Bukley | Shutterstock.com
DFree | Shutterstock.com
Ben Houdijk | Shutterstock.com

Chapter 3:

Brandon Nagy | Shutterstock.com
Drew York-Slade | Shutterstock.com
Fair Use | Wikimedia Commons
Fabio Diena | Shutterstock.com
Featureflash Photo Agency | Shutterstock.com
Mozakim | Shutterstock.com
Igor Lateci | Shutterstock.com
Kathy Hutchins | Shutterstock.com

Chapter 4:

Jamie Lamor Thompson | Shutterstock.com
Kathy Hutchins | Shutterstock.com
Ben Houdijk | Shutterstock.com
Kathy Hutchins | Shutterstock.com
Ben Houdijk | Shutterstock.com
Featureflash Photo Agency | Shutterstock.com
Lenka Horavova | Shutterstock.com
Janek Sergejev | Shutterstock.com

Chapter 5:

VGStockStudio | Shutterstock.com
Gorodenkoff | Shutterstock.com
Caddyman | Shutterstock.com
Krysja | Shutterstock.com
Nito | Shutterstock.com
Kathy Hutchins | Shutterstock.com
Ben Houdijk | Shutterstock.com
Brandon Nagy | Shutterstock.com

Front Cover:

Featureflash Photo Agency | Shutterstock.com

Video Credits

http://x-qr.net/1LLc/Sir Sammy
http://x-qr.net/1JD0/Post Malone
http://x-qr.net/1Jiq/Post Malone
http://x-qr.net/1L19/Lazy Savage
http://x-qr.net/1Kmm/Nostalgic Jams
http://x-qr.net/1LkT/Bangin' Beats
http://x-qr.net/1J9x/Daniel Krienbuehl
http://x-qr.net/1KCk/Lyric Luke
http://x-qr.net/1KBG /Nicki Swift
http://x-qr.net/1KaZ/Capital XTRA
http://x-qr.net/1Hyw/Luc Belaire
http://x-qr.net/1M1i/HOT 97
http://x-qr.net/1KGQ /VH1

Author's Biography

Carlie Lawson began writing professionally in 1991. She spent five years at a mid-sized daily newspaper, beating deadline on a daily basis while covering politics and entertainment. She has written for monthly magazines, weekly blogs, and academic publications. Educated at the University of Oklahoma, Carlie holds Bachelor's degrees in Journalism & Mass Communication, and in Film & Video Studies as well as a Master of Regional & City Planning. Carlie owns a consulting firm and conducts research in the area of natural and environmental planning. She also owns a public relations firm. She enjoys hiking, travel, reading, music, guitar, her cat, and the positive-thinking process. Learn more at https://www.writeraccess.com/writer/13038/.